Usborne
Unicorns
Puzzle Pad

Illustrated by Jenny Winstanley, Helen Graper,
Helen Prole, The Boy Fitz Hammond, Jordan Wray,
Tim Budgen, Sarah Ward and Lucy Semple

Designed by Sharon Cooper

Written by Kate Nolan

Find and circle...

...6 fireflies...

1

...7 flags...

...and 5 elves.

Can you fit the unicorns' names into the grid?

CLOUDIA   AMIRA

FIREDANCE

APELLIA

EDEN

ANYA

Each unicorn only collects flowers with a number that can be divided by the number on its bag. Circle the unicorn who will collect the most flowers.

Spot 4 differences between the pictures below.

Add up the numbers to find out how long Zephyra took to complete the course, and write the total in the final flag.

Zephyra

3.0

4.5

1.5

2.0

2.5

seconds

Can you fill in the missing vowels
to complete these unicorn words?

6

M_G_C

SP_RKL_

M_N_

G_LL_P

L_G_ND

F___RY

Can you find a nine-letter word? Move from one letter to the next along the dotted lines, using each letter only once.

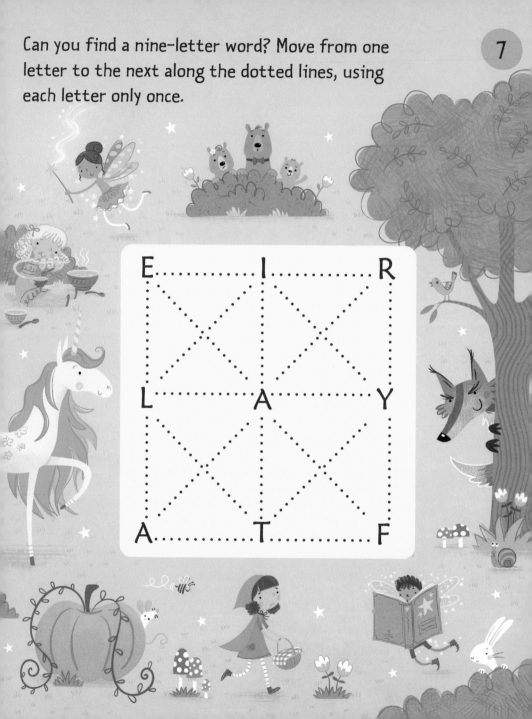

E	I	R
L	A	Y
A	T	F

Circle the 3 pieces that complete the picture.

Are there more unicorns with a pink horn
or pink hooves?

9

Can you find all the tree names in the grid?

```
S  N  O  H  A  Z  E  L  E  R
T  S  U  F  C  H  O  A  K  C
E  H  Y  G  L  S  W  O  L  H
Y  A  U  C  H  N  I  D  B  E
P  E  L  E  A  S  L  A  E  S
M  Y  W  L  L  M  L  H  E  T
J  L  T  D  T  Y  O  S  C  N
R  L  P  E  A  D  W  R  H  U
Y  O  A  R  Y  H  O  B  E  T
A  H  R  O  W  A  N  U  R  L
```

BEECH   ELDER

OAK   CHESTNUT

HAZEL   SYCAMORE

ROWAN   WILLOW

YEW   HOLLY

The more starberries the unicorns eat, the longer it takes them to get down their paths. Circle the unicorn who will eat the fewest berries and get to the end of their path first.

Spot 4 differences between the pictures below.

Can you find and circle 9 rainbow apples?

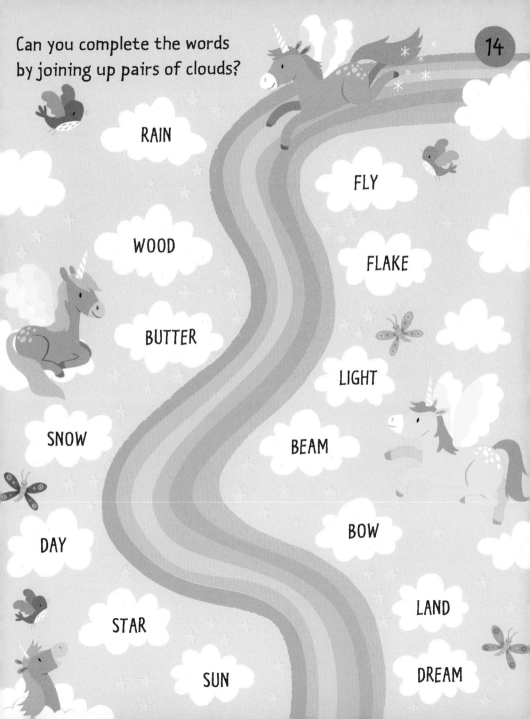

Can you complete the words
by joining up pairs of clouds?

RAIN

FLY

WOOD

FLAKE

BUTTER

LIGHT

SNOW

BEAM

DAY

BOW

LAND

STAR

DREAM

SUN

Meadow is going to meet Moonflower, but whichever way she goes, there are obstacles that add time to her journey. Draw along the quickest route.

Rainbow pool = 15 seconds   Toadstool patch = 20 seconds

Meadow

Moonflower

Fill in the shapes that have orange
spots to see the hidden picture.

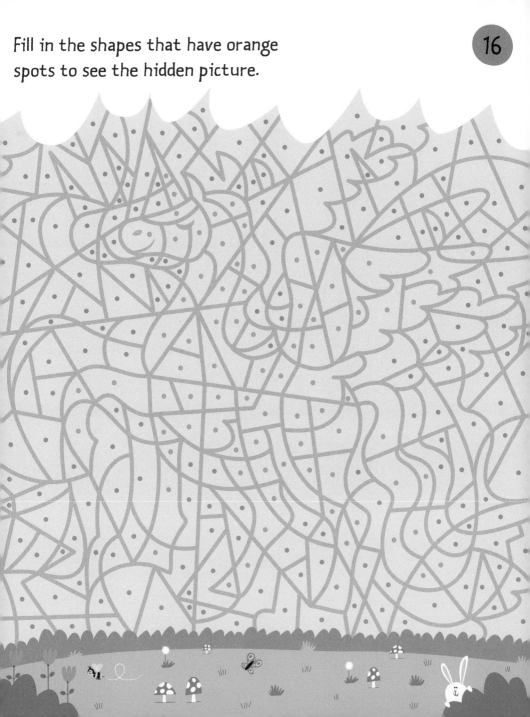

Can you spot the picture that is different from the others?

Guide Starlight across the stepping stones to meet Sylvia.

Starlight

Sylvia

Can you help the fairies finish the cupcakes by drawing on the decorations? The numbers on the jars tell you how many of each decoration can be used, and each cake must have the same amount.

15 Sprinkles

9 JELLY BEANS

3 Candy Canes

6 Starberries

6 Fairy Flowers

At the bottom of the page, circle the group of stars that the unicorns have spotted in the night sky.

Fill in the grid so that all four symbols
appear in every row and column.

The sign on each item tells you its price in spangles.
3 different items cost 20 spangles altogether.
Which ones are they?

Hoof warmers
11

Cupcakes
3

Crowns
20

Magic toadstools
1

Mirrors
17

Brushes
7

Stars
18

Rainbow carrots
4

Rainbow apples
6

Unicorn potions
14

Horseshoes
19

Can you help the unicorns find out which gemstones are in each bowl by unscrambling the letters on the labels?

SRIUBE

MAIDSNOD

DREAMSEL

SPRALE

SPOLA

Find and circle 8 lily pads...

...6 toadstools...

...4 bees...

...and 3 frogs.

Can you spot the only star in the sky with six points?

Draw a path through the toadstools for Tom and Talia. At each row, they can only pass between toadstools with odd numbers of spots.

Which silhouette matches these unicorns picking flowers?

1.

2.

3.

Can you find Claribelle's crown?

Claribelle

Guide the unicorns through the spooky forest to the castle, avoiding goblins along the way.

Find the number patterns on these strings of bunting, then add the missing numbers to the empty flags.

31

2 4 8

20 15 10

3 12

Look at the things on the shelves for one minute, then turn over and circle the ones you remember.

32

Magical Manes and
Tip-Top Tails

Look at the other side of this page
to find out how to do this puzzle.

Circle Yola's unicorn. She has a purple horn and a bow, but no flowers in her mane.

Yola

Connect the even-numbered dots in number
order to see who's in the meadow with Molly.

Molly

Find the path that will lead Azura
to the castle in the clouds.

Can you spot 13 mistakes in this unicorn story?

Once upon a tim, there was a unicorn calld Thora, who lived in a magical castel high up in the clowds. Life in the castle with the uther unicorns wos very peaseful. Evry day, they

played together. At night, thay would watch shooting stars befor bedtime. But Thora longed to sea what was beyond the castle walls, so won day, she soared away, seeking advencher...

It's bedtime, so Zarina is rounding up the unicorn foals. It takes 5 seconds to fetch each one that is standing up, and 15 seconds for each one that's lying down. How long will it take to round up all the foals outside the stable?

Zarina

Find these two groups in the picture below.

Can you fit these weather words into the grid?

SNOW

CLOUD

RAIN

RAINBOW

MIST

SUNSHINE

Can you help Hettie find her way back to her friends?

40

Hettie

In this grid, the numbers in every 3-square row, column and diagonal must add up to 15. Write the missing numbers in the empty squares.

Spot 4 differences between the pictures below.

It's bedtime, but 7 of the unicorn foals are hiding. Can you find and circle each one?

Use the clues to find out which unicorn is which, then write the correct name on each sign.

1. Juniper has a striped tail.
2. Marilla has orange hooves.
3. Sparkles is standing up.
4. Caspian has a blue mane.

Circle the 3 pieces that complete the picture.

Add spots to the empty toadstools so the spots along each side of the triangle add up to 20. Each one must have between 1 and 9 spots, and none of them should have the same amount.

Are there enough magic gems in the caves for each unicorn to collect four?

If 6 unicorns can eat 4 sacks of Sparkle Snacks, and 10 foals can eat 2 sacks, how many sacks can 3 unicorns and 5 foals eat?

....

Can you write the unicorns' names on the signs?

- Cloud is next to Lena, who has flowers in her mane.
- The rainbow apples are in front of Arrow's stall.
- Bonnie is between Chip (the smallest unicorn) and Skye.

Which of the unicorn foals at the bottom of the page comes next in the sequence?

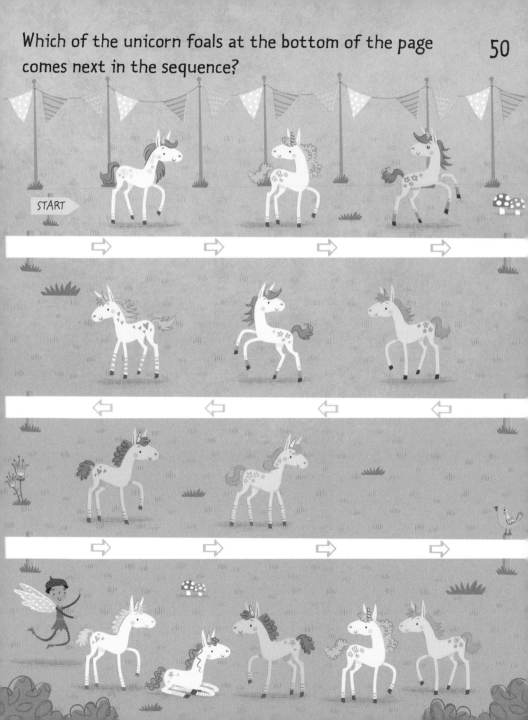

START

Circle the photo that has just been taken.

The fairy princess can take two passengers in her carriage. How many trips will she need to make so that all the fairies in the park can have a moonlit ride?

Fairy Princess's Moonlit Carriage Rides

Fill in the blank squares so that each block, row and column contains all six letters of the word FOREST.

E	R				S
F			O		
				O	
	T	E			
F	O	R		S	T
T	E				O

Can you find all of these unicorn treats in the grid?

```
S C A C O R N S P F
B T A F N U T S E A
S H A N L S A P A I
L A P B D N C C C R
A E P F E Y H A H Y
T L L S N R C K E C
E O E R T Y R A S A
P R S Z A D W I N K
S P R O U T S I E E
A C A R R O T S R S
```

APPLES   BERRIES   PETALS
FAIRY CAKE   ACORNS
CARROTS   CANDY CANE   SPROUTS
PEACHES   NUTS

Find and circle 5 rainbow apples,
3 owls and a magic wand.

Follow the trails to the stalls to find out each unicorn's name.

Deva

Spirit

Zuri

Can you spot the only unicorn without a twin?

How many bottles of potion can be made from the ingredients on the table? Write your answer on the scroll.

Recipe for an invisibility potion
(per bottle)

1 fairy toadstool
3 drops of dew
1 phoenix feather
1 starberry flower
2 teaspoons pixie dust
1 puff dragon breath
2 mermaid scales

Invisibility potion

.... bottles

Mermaid Scales

This jar contains 8 scales.

Starberry flowers

Fairy toadstools

Gathered in the unicorn forest

This bottle contains 20 drops.

Drops of dew

WARNING: VERY HOT

Pixie Dust

This bowl contains 6 teaspoons.

Phoenix feathers

Dragon Breath

This jar contains 5 puffs.

Read the descriptions below, then draw a line to match each unicorn to the name that you think suits it best.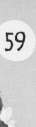

Crystal lives in a sparkling ice castle.

Starshine loves to gallop when the moon is full.

Posy frolics in flowery meadows in spring.

Storm can control the weather with her horn.

Spot 4 differences between the pictures below.

The winner of this party game has striped tights and pink shoes, but no hat. Who is it?

PIN THE HORN ON THE UNICORN

Leo

Lucy

Karina

Bob

Can you find the fairy tale characters in the grid?

```
S K O H Y Z A L E J
L G R E T E L N K A
G A O D R F W O F C
R B E A N S T A L K
A D L E T P R F H I
N L W S H S O L A E
D O J C W Z L S N I
M R T D U O L K S L
A I P M A I L U E T
W T N A I G N F L R
```

GRETEL   HANSEL   TROLL   GIANT

WITCH   GOATS   BEANSTALK

JACK   WOLF

GRANDMA

Draw the way through this sky racecourse, moving from square to square in the sequence shown at the bottom. You can't move diagonally, or go through any box twice.

63

START

FINISH

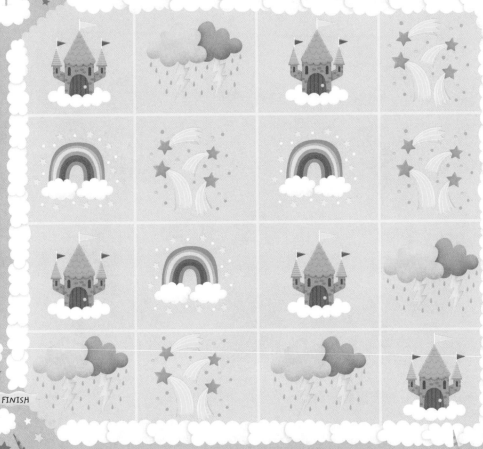

Help Ava and Adam find Carrie's cabin.
Its door number can be divided by 2, 3, 6 and 9.

For every rainbow apple that Dancer picks, Rosehip picks two. How many apples will each unicorn pick from the trees?

Dancer: .... Rosehip: ....

Dancer

Rosehip

Help Fernando the fairy finish his magic painting by shading every shape that has a blue spot.

Complete these magical jokes by matching
the questions with their punchlines.

What do you
call a unicorn
with no horn?

What did the sea say
to the mermaid?

What do you
call a wizard
on a plane?

What stories
do unicorns
like best?

What do fairies
learn at school?

Fairy tails

A flying sorcerer

The elfabet

A horse

Nothing, it
just waved.

How many 'bouquets of the day' can Petal and Blossom make from the flowers in the field?

Petal & Blossom's Flowers

Bouquet of the day!

Petal

Blossom

Find a route for Lilabelle to look at every butterfly and finish where she started, without crossing her own path.

Lilabelle

Fill in the grid so that all four symbols
appear in every row and column.

Find all the unicorns' names in the grid.

```
R  N  O  T  S  I  L  V  E  R
S  S  U  F  C  H  A  I  C  A
E  H  H  G  L  N  A  O  L  M
V  A  U  I  W  A  W  D  H  Y
O  D  L  X  R  S  S  A  O  E
M  O  O  N  L  I  G  H  T  W
J  W  Y  I  I  O  N  S  A  O
A  S  P  U  A  M  I  U  P  P
Y  I  P  N  Y  H  O  B  T  A
A  M  E  T  H  Y  S  T  H  L
```

Moonlight   Opal   Cowslip   Jaya   Silver
Amethyst   Lily   Shadow   Flash

Fill in the grid so that all four symbols
appear in every row and column.

Circle the cupcake that is different from all the others at the fairy bakery.

The numbers in this square go up in a pattern. Can you find the pattern and fill in the empty boxes?

	8		16	24
28		40		48
	56		68	
76				96
	104	112		120
124	132	140		

Can you draw 6 stars in the grid without putting 3 in a row in any direction?

Match up the words with opposite meanings.
Which toadstool isn't one of a pair?

SUMMER

NORTH

NIGHT

DARK

OLD

WINTER

DAY

SOUTH

LIGHT

NEW

QUIET

Circle the 4 pieces that complete the picture.

Add up the numbers to find out how many
seconds each unicorn takes in the rainbow race.
Who will be the first to reach the wishing well?

Amber

Buttercup

4

3

5

6

4

2

1

7

3

1

7

5

2

3

Spot 5 differences between the pictures below.

Which unicorn will reach the wishing well?

Ruby

Kilana

Logan

Are there enough shooting stars
for each fairy to catch three?

Match up the fairies to their unicorns.
Which fairy won't be riding today?

UNICORN
& FAIRY
SHOW DAY

Solve the calculations to find out how strong the unicorns' magic powers are, then add them up and circle the most powerful unicorn.

Fern

Healing:	17 + 13 =
Speed:	9 x 5 =
Invisibility:	40 ÷ 10 =
Total power:	

Ben

Healing:	50 - 30 =
Speed:	80 ÷ 2 =
Invisibility:	13 + 5 =
Total power:	

Monty

Healing:	6 x 10 =
Speed:	27 - 15 =
Invisibility:	10 ÷ 2 =
Total power:	

Valeria

Healing:	16 + 9 =
Speed:	12 x 2 =
Invisibility:	40 - 9 =
Total power:	

Circle the photo that has just been taken.

Fill in the blank clouds, so that each number is the sum of the two directly beneath it.

Which path should Petal take to put the star on top of the Christmas tree?

Petal

Connect the odd-numbered dots in number order to see who's exploring the coral reef.

Draw stars on 4 of the unicorns' blankets, hearts on half of the remaining ones, and stripes on half of the rest. How many are left with plain blankets?

Can you spot the unicorn that is different from all
the rest at the toy shop?

Unicorn
Toy Shop

Circle the unicorn foal who isn't joined to a fairy.

UNICORN
TRAINING

Can you find out where each basket of rainbow apples should be delivered? Do the calculations, then draw a line between each tag and its matching stable.

1/2 of 14

1/4 of 8

21-18

95-91

35-29

1/5 of 25

Can you find these mythical creatures in the grid?

```
S R O H Y Z A L E R
G A D R A G O N K P
R O I D R S W O L I
I A C P H O E N I X
F D L E E S L L E I
F L W S N T L A F E
I O J B P T I T C I
N E M O N G A R L X
M E R M A I D U P S
L H R O F T N S R S
```

ELF   PHOENIX
PIXIE   GRIFFIN
MERMAID   FAIRY
CENTAUR   GNOME
DRAGON   SPRITE

Circle the unicorn that matches the silhouette.

Use the clues to find out what each unicorn will get from the Snack Shack, and draw a line to match them up.

Circle the 3 pieces that complete the picture. 96

Divide the field into seven areas by drawing fences. Each area must contain the same number of squares as rainbow carrots. The first carrot has been fenced in already.

Follow the sparkly trails to find out who set off each magic firework.

Circle 4 pink flags, 2 balloons, a butterfly and a dog.

Can you circle these 5 parts of the picture?

Use the symbols below to help you finish this joke:
How do bees brush their hair?

THEY USE A

HONEYCOMB

Each unicorn needs two apples and three carrots.
How many of each are needed altogether?

Apples: ....   Carrots: ....

Can you circle these 5 parts of the picture?

Help Tilly find her way through the toadstools
to reach the fairies in the middle.

Tilly

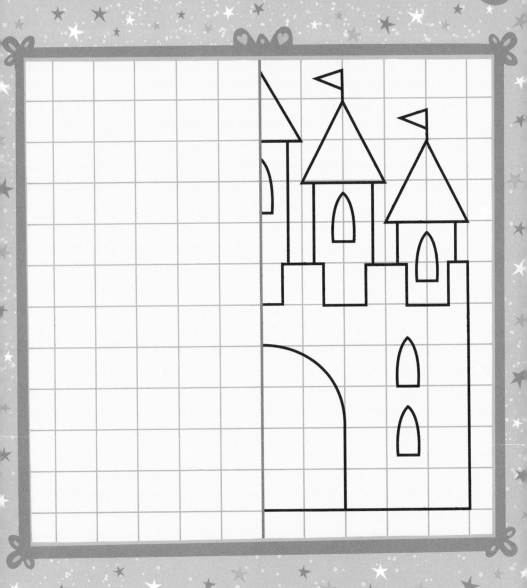

Are there more sea unicorns
or unicorn seahorses?

Spot 5 differences between the pictures below.

The fastest time ever galloped on the rainbow racetrack is 1 minute and 29 seconds. Add up Flossy's times on the flags. Has she beaten the record? Circle yes or no.

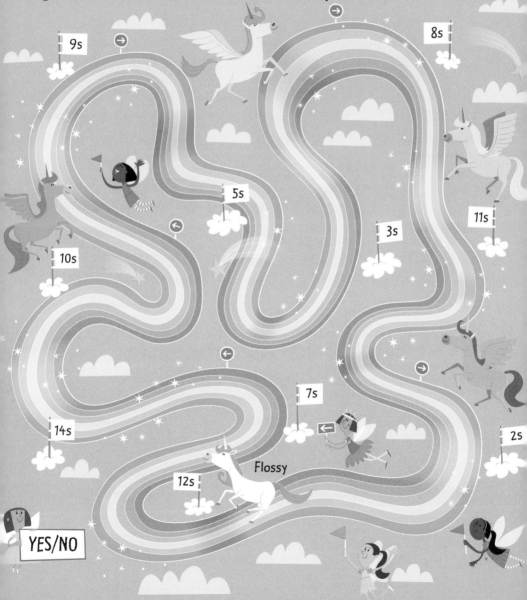

9s

8s

5s

3s

11s

10s

7s

14s

2s

12s

Flossy

YES/NO

If all the unicorns follow these instructions, which one will reach the wishing well?

1 square forward, 1 square north, 2 squares west,
3 squares south, 1 square east, 1 square south,
2 squares east, 2 squares north

The grid below is made up of 9 blocks, each with 9 squares. Fill in the blank squares so that every block, row and column contains all the digits 1 to 9.

6		9	1			5	4	7
	4	1		6			8	
5	2		7		4		9	6
1			8		3		6	9
8	9	4	6	5		3	2	1
		6	4	1		7	5	8
3		8	2	4				
		5		6	8	3	4	
4		5	3	9	8	6	1	

Which silhouette matches this row of unicorns?

1.

2.

3.

Connie

Phina

Damia

Help Celesta find her way through the snowy mountains to the castle, avoiding any cracks in the ice.

113

Celesta

Write a word on each leaf that can be made by changing just one letter of the word before it. There is a clue on each leaf to help you.

MOON

Another word for a grumble

Not very kind

What Jack planted

BEAM

Cross out every letter that is one of
a pair. What word can you spell with
the five letters that are left?

Spot 4 differences between the pictures below.

Find out who scored the most points at the Unicorn Games by filling in the missing numbers, then write 1st, 2nd, 3rd or 4th on the dotted lines below each column.

THE UNICORN GAMES
· RESULTS ·

	Violet	Irina	Rainbow	Frank	Total
Cloud jumping	3	5	4	2	
Spell casting	5	3		6	20
Raindrop race		4		5	
Total score	16		19		

Violet

Irina

Rainbow

Frank

Circle 16 snowballs, 9 toadstools and 2 rainbow carrots.

In the unicorn show, Berry finished ahead of Floriana but behind Pippin. Yasmin finished behind Pippin but ahead of Berry. Write 1st, 2nd, 3rd or 4th in each unicorn's rosette.

7

1st

Winner

Unicorn Show

Floriana

Yasmin

Berry

Pippin

DER

NEREG

GOIDIN

GEROAN

TIVOLE

LEWOYL

EUBL

The unicorns have been picking starberries.

- Hazel picked 3 times as many as Daisy.
- Moonbeam collected 18 berries (8 more than Alfie).
- Daisy picked half as many as Alfie.

Next to their names, write how many berries each one picked.

Hazel: ....

Moonbeam: ....

Daisy: ....

Alfie: ....

Luna is lost in the spooky forest, and she needs your help to escape. Use the key to find out what to do at each obstacle.

KEY

Go north from bats.

Go south from ghosts.

Go west from swamps.

Go east from toadstools.

Luna

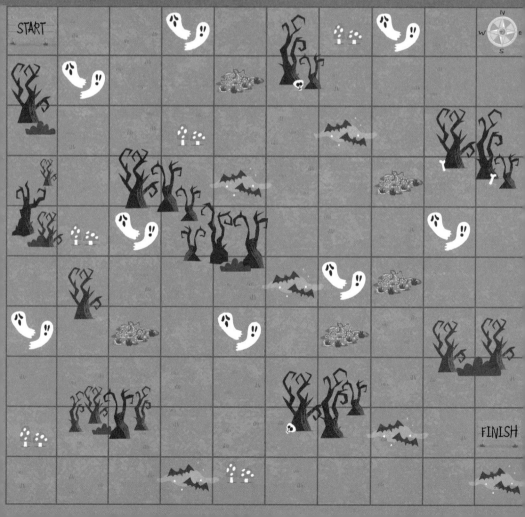

START

FINISH

Find these two groups in the picture below.

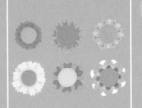

Help Firefly find her way through the clouds to the rainbow.

Firefly

Each of these unicorns needs a set of magic unicorn shoes. How many shoes will Felix the fairy have to make?

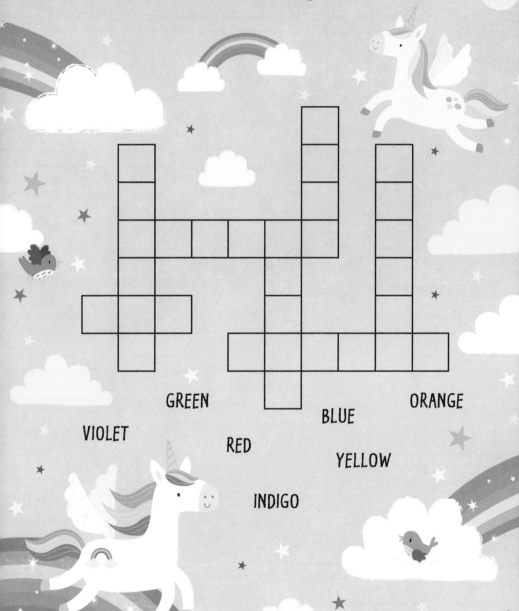

GREEN

VIOLET

ORANGE

BLUE

RED

YELLOW

INDIGO

This grid is made up of 6 blocks, each with 6 squares. Fill in the blank squares so that each block, row and column contains all the digits 1 to 6.

	1			3	2
			5		1
		3		4	
	5	6		2	
5					
2	6				

In the unicorn race, Dazzle finished before Sienna, but after Sunbeam. Thunder wasn't first, but was two places in front of Leila. No unicorn beginning with 'S' came last. Write the unicorns' names on the scoreboard below.

Sunbeam

Dazzle

Leila

Sienna

Thunder

SCOREBOARD

1st..

2nd.................... 3rd....................

4th.................... 5th....................

1st

Find these two groups in the picture below.

Fill in the grid so all the letters in the word
HORN appear in every row and column.

	R		H
		O	
		R	
	N		O

Are there enough rainbow carrots for
each unicorn to have one?

Find and circle the unicorn picture that is different from all the others.

Spot 4 differences between the pictures below.

Solve the clues to fill in the blank spaces below.

ACROSS

2. Enchantment (5)
5. A witch may ride this (10)
8. A four-leaf ____ may be lucky (6)
9. Male magician or sorcerer (6)
10. Little bearded man often seen in gardens (5)
11. Magic stick (4)
12. If something is ____ it cannot be seen (9)

DOWN

1. Witch's purring pet (5, 3)
3. Magic liquid (6)
4. It's worn on a horse's foot, and some think it's lucky (9)
6. 3 downs can be made in this big, black pot (8)
7. A unicorn has just one (4)
9. Dragons, fairies and phoenixes all have these (5)

Fill in the shapes that have pink spots to see the hidden picture.

Can you circle these 5 parts of the picture?

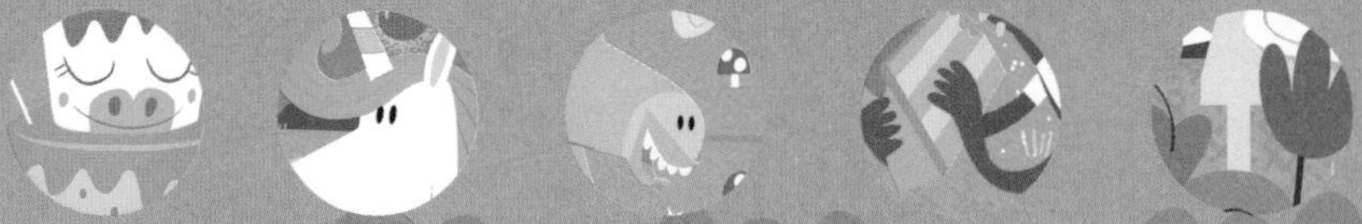

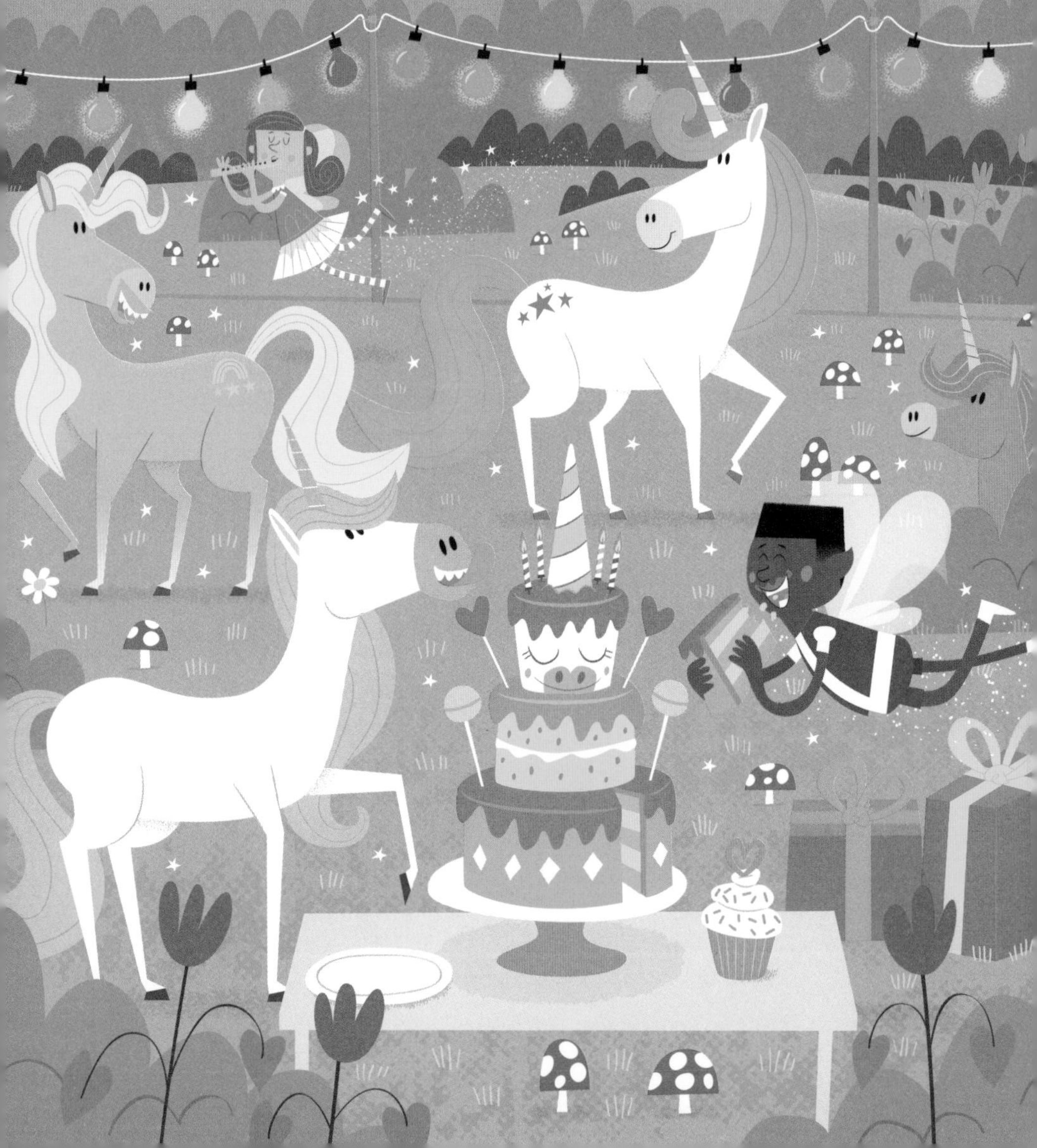

Circle the words that can't be made with letters from the word FLOWERS. Each letter can be used only once.

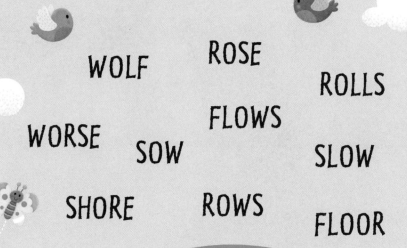

WOLF

ROSE

ROLLS

FLOWS

WORSE

SOW

SLOW

SHORE

ROWS

FLOOR

Answers

1

2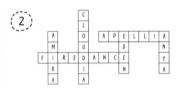

3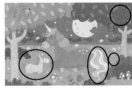

5 13.5 seconds

6 MAGIC, SPARKLE, MANE, GALLOP, LEGEND, FAIRY

7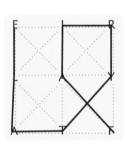

FAIRY-TALE

9 Pink hooves
(5 with a pink horn,
6 with pink hooves)

10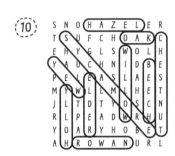

11

4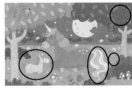

8

12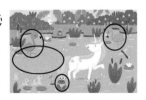

Answers

13

16

19 Each cake should
have 5 sprinkles,
3 jelly beans, 1
candy cane, 2
starberries and
2 fairy flowers.

14 RAIN – BOW
WOOD – LAND
BUTTER – FLY
SNOW – FLAKE
DAY – DREAM
STAR – LIGHT
SUN – BEAM

17

20

21

15

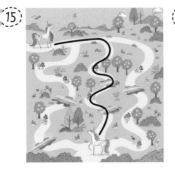

18

22 Hoof warmers,
a rainbow apple
and a cupcake

Answers

(23) RUBIES, DIAMONDS,
EMERALDS,
PEARLS, OPALS

(26)

(29)

(24)

(27)

(30)

(25)

(28) 3

(31) 2, 4, 6, 8, 10
25, 20, 15, 10, 5
3, 6, 9, 12, 15

Answers

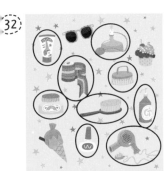
(32)

(35)

(39)

	C										
	L			M			R	A	I	N	
	O			I			A				
S	U	N	S	H	I	N	E				
	D			T			N				
				N			B				
				O			O				
	S	N	O	W							

(33)

(36) Once upon a **time**, there was a unicorn **called** Thora, who lived in a magical **castle** high up in the **clouds**. Life in the castle with the **other** unicorns **was** very **peaceful**. **Every** day, they played to-gether. At night, **they** would watch shooting stars **before** bedtime. But Thora longed to **see** what was beyond the castle walls, so **one** day, she soared away, seeking **adventure**...

(40)
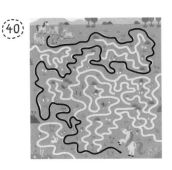

(37) 45 seconds

(34)

(38)
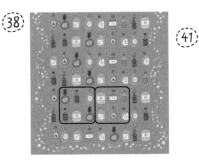

(41)

Answers

(42)

(45)

(48)

3 sacks

(46)

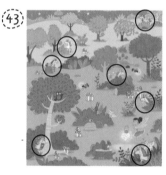
(43)

(49)

(47)

Yes. There are
16 gems for 4
unicorns.

(44)

(50)

Answers

51

54
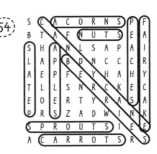

57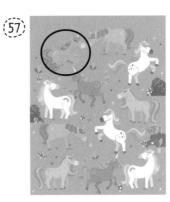

52

3 trips

55

58

3
bottles

53

E	R	O	F	T	S
S	F	T	O	E	R
R	S	F	T	O	E
O	T	E	S	R	F
F	O	R	E	S	T
T	E	S	R	F	O

56

59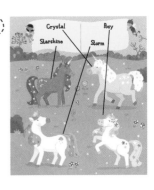

Answers

 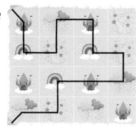

Karina

67. What do you call a
unicorn with no horn?
A horse
What did the sea say
to the mermaid?
Nothing, it just waved.
What do fairies learn
at school?
The elfabet
What do you call a
wizard on a plane?
A flying sorcerer
What stories do
unicorns like best?
Fairy tails

Dancer: 7
Rosehip: 14

5 bouquets

Answers

69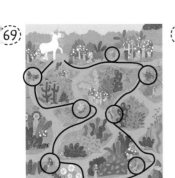

72

75

or:

76 SUMMER – WINTER
NORTH – SOUTH
LIGHT – DARK
DAY – NIGHT
OLD – NEW
QUIET is not
one of a pair.

70

73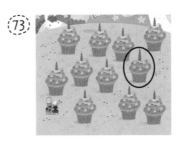

77

71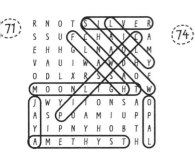

74

4	8	12	16	20	24
28	32	36	40	44	48
52	56	60	64	68	72
76	80	84	88	92	96
100	104	108	112	116	120
124	128	132	136	140	144

78 Buttercup wins.
(Buttercup 25:
Amber 28)

Answers

(79)

(80)

Logan

(81) No. There are 4 fairies and 10 shooting stars.

(82)

(83)

30 + 45 + 4 = 79
20 + 40 + 18 = 78
60 + 12 + 5 = 77
25 + 24 + 31 = 80

(84)

(85)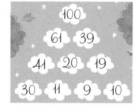

100
61 39
41 20 19
30 11 9 10

(86)

(87)

(88) 2
(4 with stars,
4 with hearts,
2 striped)

(89)

(90) RUBY, AMBER,
MOONSTONE,
SAPPHIRE, OPAL,
TOPAZ,
DIAMOND, JADE

Answers

91

94

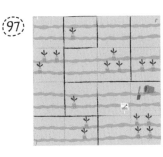

97

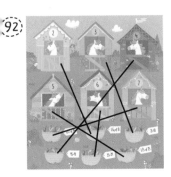

92

95

98

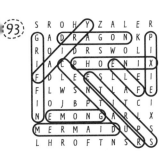

93

96

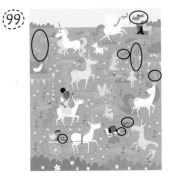

99

Answers

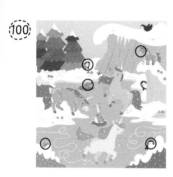

100

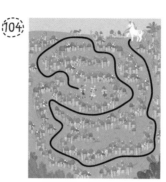

104

107

101 They use a honeycomb.

105

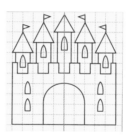

108

Yes

(1 min 21 secs)

102 Apples: 12
Carrots: 18

103

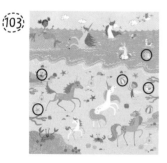

106 More unicorn seahorses
(4 sea unicorns:
7 unicorn seahorses)

109

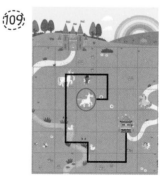

Answers

110

6	8	9	1	3	2	5	4	7
7	4	1	9	6	5	2	8	3
5	2	3	7	8	4	1	9	6
1	5	7	8	2	3	4	6	9
8	9	4	6	5	7	3	2	1
2	3	6	4	1	9	7	5	8
3	6	8	2	4	1	9	7	5
9	1	2	5	7	6	8	3	4
4	7	5	3	9	8	6	1	2

113

114

MOON, MOAN, MEAN, BEAN, BEAM

111

2

115

MAGIC

112

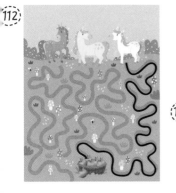

116

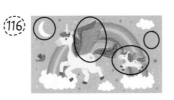

117

	Violet	Irina	Rainbow	Frank	Total
Cloud jumping	3	5	4	2	14
Spell casting	5	3	6	6	20
Raindrop race	8	4	9	5	26
Total score	16	12	19	13	60
	2nd	4th	1st	3rd	

118

119

1st: Pippin
2nd: Yasmin
3rd: Berry
4th: Floriana

Answers

120

RED
GREEN
INDIGO
ORANGE
VIOLET
YELLOW
BLUE

123

127

6	1	5	4	3	2
3	4	2	5	6	1
1	2	3	6	4	5
4	5	6	1	2	3
5	3	4	2	1	6
2	6	1	3	5	4

128 1st: Sunbeam
     2nd: Dazzle
     3rd: Thunder
     4th: Sienna
     5th: Leila

124

121 Hazel: 15
     Daisy: 5
     Moonbeam: 18
     Alfie: 10

125 28 shoes

129
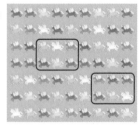

122

126

```
            B
            L
  V         U         I
  I         E         N
  O R A N G E         D
  L         R         I
R E D       E         G
  T       Y E L L O W
            N
```

130

O	R	N	H
N	H	O	R
H	O	R	N
R	N	H	O

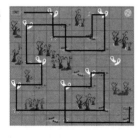

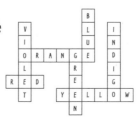